CONTENTS

Back cover One of the Stirling Heads, oak carvings that decorated a ceiling in the Palace.
This page A weapon used during the Radical War of 1820.

WELCOME TO STIRLING CASTLE

This was a major fortification and royal residence from at least the 1100s. It occupies a strategic position, overlooking a key crossing point of the River Forth, and was a crucial stronghold throughout the Wars of Independence of 1296–1357, and long afterwards.

From the late 1400s, the Stewart monarchs developed Stirling as a prestigious Renaissance residence.

James IV's Great Hall is probably the finest banqueting hall ever built in Scotland. The Palace built for James V and Queen Mary of Guise ranks among the most ambitious in Britain. And the Chapel Royal added by James VI is Scotland's grandest purpose-built Protestant chapel.

After James VI became James I of England in 1603, Stirling Castle declined as a royal centre, but its military functions expanded and for well over a century it was the

1 An aerial view of the castle from the west.
2 A mermaid carving on the Great Hall.

headquarters of The Argyll and Sutherland Highlanders, whose regimental museum is housed here.

Over the past two centuries, Stirling Castle has attracted growing numbers of visitors, and their experience has been enhanced in recent decades by the recreation of the Great Hall and Palace as they may have looked during their royal heyday.

2

WHO'S WHO

KING DAVID I
(c.1085–1153)

David expanded an early royal base at Stirling, and founded Cambuskenneth Abbey nearby to provide spiritual support.

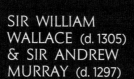

SIR WILLIAM WALLACE (d. 1305) & SIR ANDREW MURRAY (d. 1297)

Wallace and Murray led the Scots to an early victory over the English invaders at Stirling in 1297.

KING ROBERT I (THE BRUCE)
(1274–1329)

Bruce's famous victory nearby at Bannockburn in 1314 led to the removal of English occupiers from the castle. He had its defences dismantled to prevent future English occupation.

JOAN BEAUFORT
(d. 1445)

Queen Joan brought her son James II to Stirling after the assassination of her husband, James I, and for two years ruled Scotland as regent.

JAMES II
(1430–60)

As King of Scots, James made extensive use of his royal castle at Stirling, most notoriously when he killed the Earl of Douglas during a brawl here in 1452.

MARY OF GUELDERS
(d. 1463)

The daughter of a Low Countries duke and duchess, Mary, above, married James II to become Queen of Scots, and after his death governed Scotland as regent. Famously pious, she distributed alms to the poor at Stirling.

MARGARET OF DENMARK
(c.1457–86)

Born a Scandinavian princess, as Queen consort of Scotland, Margaret, right, established her court here at Stirling with her children, and was widely admired for her wisdom.

JAMES IV
(1473–1513)

The most dynamic of the Stewart monarchs, James developed Stirling as a Renaissance castle, commissioning the vast Great Hall and the King's Old Building as his residence.

WHO'S WHO

JAMES V
(1512–42)

James commissioned Stirling's magnificent Palace as a fitting home for his French wife Mary of Guise, but died without ever meeting his daughter and successor Mary Queen of Scots.

MARY QUEEN OF SCOTS
(1542–87)

Born at Linlithgow, Queen Mary spent most of her early childhood in the more secure stronghold of Stirling Castle. It was also an important residence during her adult reign.

JAMES VI
(1566–1625)

After becoming king at 13 months old, James was largely raised at Stirling. He commissioned the Chapel Royal in 1594 for the baptism of his heir, Prince Henry.

ANNABELLA MURRAY, COUNTESS OF MAR
(1536–1603)

As custodian of both the infant James VI and his eldest son, Prince Henry, Lady Mar ran a large royal household at Stirling Castle.

JOHN ERSKINE, 6TH EARL OF MAR
(1674/5–1732)

The hereditary governor of Stirling Castle, Mar is best known for raising a Jacobite army in 1715. His military failures later that year led to exile in France.

THE ARGYLL AND SUTHERLAND HIGHLANDERS
(1881–2006)

One of the British Army's great Highland regiments, based here from its inception until 2006. The regimental museum is here at the castle.

JANE FERRIER
(1767–1846)

After marrying the deputy governor of the castle, artist Ferrier produced many illustrations, including detailed drawings of the Stirling Heads, which she published in 1817.

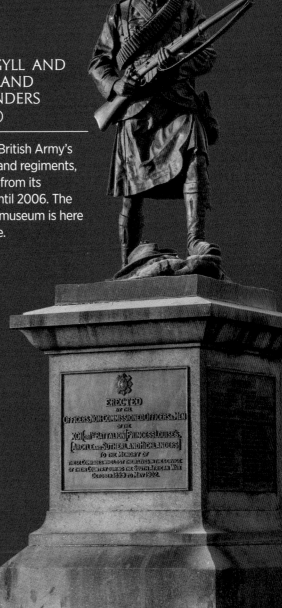

ERECTED
BY THE
OFFICERS, NON COMMISSIONED OFFICERS & MEN
OF THE
XCI OR I ST BATTALION PRINCESS LOUISE'S,
ARGYLE AND SUTHERLAND HIGHLANDERS
TO THE MEMORY OF
THESE COMRADES WHO LOST THEIR LIVES IN THE SERVICE
OF THEIR COUNTRY DURING THE SOUTH AFRICAN WAR
OCTOBER 1899 TO MAY 1902.

EXPLORING THE CASTLE

We recommend visiting the castle's buildings in the order they appear here – but you are free to explore as you wish.

A good place to start is the Castle Exhibition, which is accessed via the Queen Anne Garden, and gives a broad introduction to the castle's history.

The most important buildings – the Palace, King's Old Building, Chapel Royal and Great Hall – are grouped around the Inner Close at the highest point on the rock.

However, visitors normally enter the Palace from the Outer Close. Allow plenty of time to explore this splendid Renaissance residence. It has been lavishly recreated as it may have looked in the 1540s, soon after the Palace was completed. Costumed interpreters can usually be found inside these rooms and will be happy to tell you about the royal court at Stirling.

Other highlights to discover include the Regimental Museum of The Argyll and Sutherland Highlanders, the recreated Castle Kitchens and, at the far end of the Nether Bailey, the Tapestry Exhibition.

This page The Forework, with the Great Hall behind and the Palace at the left.

OUTER DEFENCES

The wall facing you as you approach from the Esplanade, and the ditch in front of it, were built from 1708, a new first line of defence for the castle.

By the early 1700s, there was a new threat of civil war between government forces and the Jacobites, who wanted to replace Queen Anne with her Catholic brother Prince James Francis Edward.

The new defences were designed by Captain Theodore Dury, one of the leading military engineers of his day.

From the Esplanade, you can see many of the castle's structures.

❶ Pepperpot sentry box
Part of Dury's defences, providing basic shelter from gunfire and from the elements.

❷ Boer War memorial
Depicting a soldier of the Argyll and Sutherland Highlanders.

❸ Entrance
The main route into the castle from the 1700s, originally accessed by a drawbridge.

❹ Prince's Tower
Part of the Forework added for James IV around 1500; later incorporated into the Palace.

5 Palace
The prestigious royal residence built for James V and Mary of Guise in the 1530s–40s.

6 Ditch
A hazard for attackers, with gunholes for cannon and muskets.

7 Overport Battery
An L-shaped row of gun emplacements; a key part of Dury's defences.

8 Great Hall
A magnificent royal reception room completed in 1503.

9 Main Guard House and Fort Major's House
Built in the late 1700s, these buildings now contain a gift shop and offices.

10 French Spur
An artillery defence added by Mary of Guise's engineers in the 1540s.

11 Robert the Bruce statue
Sculpted by Andrew Currie in 1876, the statue faces Bannockburn, scene of Bruce's great military victory.

THE FOREWORK

Commissioned by James IV around 1500, for two centuries the Forework was the outward face of the castle.

It greeted visitors from the south – the usual approach to the castle – with a display of opulence and defensive might, proclaiming James as a powerful and cultured monarch.

A description of about 1582 refers to the four rounded towers flanking the entrance as 'the whole outward beauty of the place'. At that time, they and the gatehouse linking them stood five storeys tall. A wooden bridge led up to the triple doors, each fitted with a portcullis.

Around 1712, the two outer gatehouse towers were demolished – though the lowest part of the west tower survives, overlooking the Queen Anne Garden. The two inner towers were reduced to their present height to act as gun platforms. Even in its reduced state, this is an impressive ceremonial entrance.

The Forework façade terminated in a rectangular tower at each end. The larger eastern tower was probably home to the constable, a senior court official who managed the castle. It is called the Elphinstone Tower, after the man who held this post in 1508.

It was reduced in the late 1600s to create a gun platform, but you can still enter and explore the lower floors.

The Prince's Tower at the west end was incorporated into the Palace in the 1530s (see page 36).

1 The Forework as it may have looked when completed around 1500.
2 Reduced but still impressive: the Forework today.

THE QUEEN ANNE GARDEN

The quiet and attractive garden below the towering walls of the Palace is named after the last Stuart monarch, who reigned 1702–14. But she never visited Stirling.

In fact, the garden may have been established much earlier, in the mid-1400s, when Scotland's kings and queens spent much of their time at Stirling. The raised terrace at the foot of the Forework wall was created soon after the Palace was completed in the 1540s.

In the 1620s, by which time the royal family had relocated to London, the garden became a bowling green, and a walkway enclosed by balusters was added.

From the Queen Anne Garden, you can access the casemates: artillery-proof storage arches behind the outer defences, where troops might be stationed during sieges. They now house the Castle Exhibition, introducing the story of the castle.

Right The Queen Anne Garden.

THE INNER AND OUTER CLOSES

Stirling Castle is divided into zones, with buildings arranged around yards or wards. As at other castles, these are grouped according to status and function.

The rocky topography of the Castle Rock dictated much of the layout and orientation of these buildings.

Outer Close
A more public space within the castle enclosure, the Outer Close is lower in both altitude and status than the Inner, but it gave controlled access to the Great Hall and the Palace, and included other important buildings such as kitchens, guardhouses and residential blocks.

Inner Close

This is the heart of the castle, at its highest point, and has probably always been the main focus of status and fortification. The earliest royal buildings of the 1100s once stood here.

The Inner Close gave elite residents access to the most important buildings: the King's Old Building, Great Hall, Palace and Chapel Royal. These were all built between 1490 and 1600, but replaced earlier buildings with similar functions.

Nether Bailey

This low-lying walled enclosure is reached via the North Gate of 1381, but probably dates back much further, to the earliest days of the castle. It never contained prestigious buildings, but was used for storage and workshops.

1

THE PALACE

This is one of Britain's finest Renaissance buildings, designed as a prestigious and luxurious home for royalty.

Stirling Palace was commissioned in 1538 by King James V, as he prepared to marry the French noblewoman Mary of Guise. He was determined to welcome her to a residence of suitable grandeur.

James died suddenly in 1542. It's unlikely the Palace was finished by then, but its completion was overseen by Mary, who made her court here.

The Palace was intended to portray James as a Renaissance 'prince': just, wealthy and powerful; the figurehead of a cultured court, steeped in Classical mythology, Christian faith and Renaissance art.

Over 200 stone figures adorned the exterior; each was probably brightly painted. Many are now badly weathered, with no trace of colour. But the surviving stonework reveals James's aspirations.

The Palace buildings are arranged around a square courtyard known as the Lion's Den, reached via a ground-floor transe or passage, where you can now visit accessible galleries and family-oriented displays.

1 The Palace.
2 The Lion's Den.

According to legend, James V kept a live lion in the Lion's Den, signifying his power and exotic tastes, and reflecting Scottish royal heraldry. The Palace's main entrance was via an external timber stair (now a modern replacement).

The interiors of the Palace rooms of the 1540s were recreated in 2001–11, a major refurbishment project underpinned by years of expert research.

The fireplaces and doorways are original; the decoration and furnishings are all replicas, based on suitable examples from elsewhere. The bright colours may seem garish to modern eyes, but are an authentic reflection of Renaissance fashions.

Inside, you may encounter costumed interpreters, who will help bring these rooms to life.

LOOK OUT BELOW

At the far end of the transe, a door leads out to the Ladies' Lookout, a grassy enclosure offering superb views west of the castle, over the royal pleasure grounds known as the King's Knot (see page 57).

SOMETHING WICKED

Look closely at the Palace's main door. Someone has carved onto it the letters AMV, for *Ave Maria Virginus* ('Hail Mary the Virgin'). This was probably intended to ward off evil but the author of the graffiti is unknown.

1

THE QUEEN'S OUTER AND INNER HALLS

The main floor of the palace contains two apartments, for the king and queen. Each apartment has an outer hall, an inner hall and a bedchamber.

As its name suggests, the **Queen's Outer Hall** was the most public of the three. It served as an anteroom for people seeking to visit the queen, and a dining room where she could entertain larger groups, with guests of highest status seated closest to her.

The wall decoration is based on a frieze of the mid-1500s at Kinneil House, 20 miles away. The windows have been glazed in a pattern of interlocking diagonal panels that was fashionable in France at that time. They incorporate the heraldry of Queen Mary of Guise.

The **Queen's Inner Hall** was a more secluded space, where the queen received courtiers and important visitors. It includes a replica chair of estate – raised on a plinth and overhung by a canopy – from which the queen could survey the room.

The walls and ceiling are very lavishly decorated. The walls are painted to look as though they are covered by red hangings – notice how the hangings are 'parted' at the doorways. The 'harebell' pattern is based on a motif carved on the fireplace in the Queen's Bedchamber.

All the carved stone fireplaces in the palace have survived, though they are no longer brightly painted.

The ceiling panels are modelled on a painted ceiling of the mid-1500s from Winchester College in Hampshire, England.

The Unicorn tapestries were commissioned specifically for this room. (See overleaf.)

1 The Queen's Outer Hall as it may have looked in the 1540s.
2 The Queen's Inner Hall.

2

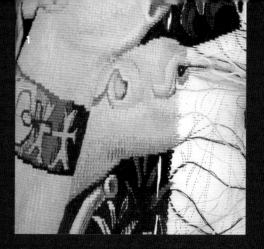

THE UNICORN TAPESTRIES

The tapestries displayed in the Queen's Lodgings were made in 2001–13, as part of a project to recreate the splendour of the Renaissance court at Stirling.

In the 1500s, tapestries were prized possessions for elite households around Europe. Monarchs bought them in large numbers to adorn their palaces, in a conspicuous show of wealth and sophistication. James V owned about 200 tapestries and hangings, some of which travelled with him when his household moved between Stirling, Holyrood, Linlithgow and other royal palaces.

James's collection included two sets of Unicorn tapestries. This mythical beast with miraculous powers held special significance in Scotland, where it featured in royal heraldry.

James's Unicorn tapestries no longer survive, so the decision was taken to commission a new set, with support from the Quinque Foundation of America. They were modelled on seven tapestries produced in the Low Countries around 1500, which are now held by the Metropolitan Museum of Art in New York.

The weavings present a narrative about huntsmen pursuing and killing a unicorn. The slaughter of the unicorn is a Christian allegory representing the Crucifixion, but the hunt may also represent romantic love.

The new tapestries were created by weavers from West Dean Tapestry Studio in Sussex, England. They studied the originals closely to produce the new designs, then worked by hand using traditional tools and materials. Three of the tapestries were woven at West Dean, the other four here at Stirling Castle (see page 55).

The Unicorn Tapestries play a key role in the recreated Renaissance Palace, providing an authentic richness of colour, detail and symbolism.

1 A partly woven detail from the tapestry
   The Unicorn Leaps Out of the Stream.
2 The same tapestry when finished.

THE QUEEN'S BEDCHAMBER

The most private room of the queen's apartment was also the most comfortable and richly decorated.

The furnishing and decoration of the Queen's Bedchamber revive the sumptuous textures, complex patterns and deep colours that were fashionable when Mary of Guise lived here in the 1540s.

❶ Chairs
Upholstered cross-frame chairs of a kind imported by James V from France.

❷ Cloth of estate
Featuring Mary of Guise's coat of arms 'impaled' or combined with the royal arms of Scotland. The same heraldry appears at the centre of the painted and gilded ceiling.

❸ Bed
Based on one owned by Mary of Guise and later inherited by her daughter, Mary Queen of Scots. The queen probably slept in a small adjoining room called a closet, which has not survived.

❹ Carpets
Expensive imports from Turkey and Persia, used on both floors and tables.

Left The Queen's Bedchamber.

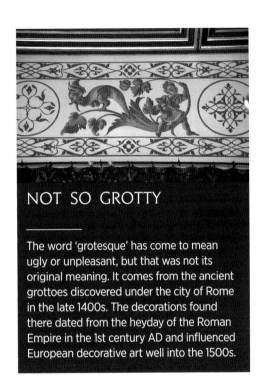

NOT SO GROTTY

The word 'grotesque' has come to mean ugly or unpleasant, but that was not its original meaning. It comes from the ancient grottoes discovered under the city of Rome in the late 1400s. The decorations found there dated from the heyday of the Roman Empire in the 1st century AD and influenced European decorative art well into the 1500s.

❺ Prayer table
Topped by a devotional triptych (three-panelled framed painting) depicting the Virgin and Child, St Cecilia and St Clare of Assisi. A personal altar like this probably stood in Mary's adjoining sleeping closet.

❻ Wall decoration
The frieze and window recesses are painted with grotesque motifs such as foliage transforming into fantastical creatures. This was highly fashionable in the 1500s.

STIRLING CORONATIONS

James V was crowned at Stirling, in the old Chapel Royal, after the death of his father James IV at Flodden in 1513. Scottish nobles who had survived the carnage flocked to the castle. They may have feared a retaliatory attack by the English and seen Stirling as a secure location.

1

In 1543 James V's daughter, Mary Queen of Scots, was also crowned in the Chapel Royal, after which there was 'bankating and great danceing befor the queen with greit lordis and frinche ladyis'.

Mary was forced to abdicate in 1567. Five days later, her son, James VI, was hurriedly crowned in Stirling's Kirk of the Holy Rude. An oath made on James's behalf promised that he would 'ruit out all Heretykis and Enemyis to the trew Wirship of God'.

1 Scotland's royal crown, created in 1540 for James V.
2 The coronation of the infant Mary Queen of Scots in 1543, when the crown had a purple bonnet.

THE KING'S BEDCHAMBER

The king's apartment mirrored the queen's. Visitors progress through its rooms from the most private to the most public.

The King's Bedchamber contains a large bed, but without elaborate bedclothes and hangings. This is because the Palace has been recreated as it may have looked after James V's death in 1542. The monarch was now his daughter, Mary Queen of Scots, but as a young child she slept elsewhere in the castle.

KNOCK KNOCK

The King's Bedchamber is linked to the Queen's by a single door. Research has revealed that it could only be locked or unlocked from her side.

In fact, the bed was not normally used for sleeping, but as an elevated seat, from which the king might welcome honoured guests. He probably slept in the cosy closet tucked behind the fireplace.

When James was alive, this room would have been splendidly decorated and furnished. This is indicated by the colourful and elaborate ceiling with its heraldic motifs, plaster mouldings and gilding.

THE KING'S INNER AND OUTER HALLS

Proceeding from the King's Bedchamber are two further rooms, where the king engaged with courtiers and visitors. They include some of the Palace's most spectacular decoration.

The **King's Inner Hall**, like the queen's, was used for meetings of advisors and for more intimate meals. It would have contained a chair of estate, raised on a platform and overhung by a canopy, where the king could sit to receive visitors.

This room features one of the most spectacular decorative features of the Palace: the Stirling Heads. These oak carvings are discussed in more detail on pages 30–33. The walls are muted by comparison, painted in grey tones, with elaborate motifs modelled on those in Mary Queen of Scots' apartments at the Palace of Holyroodhouse in Edinburgh.

ROOM WITH A LOOM

The first of the Stirling Tapestries, *The Unicorn in Captivity*, was woven in the King's Outer Hall in 2001–3. After this, work began to recreate the room and the weavers moved to the purpose-built studio in the Nether Bailey (see page 55).

The **King's Outer Hall** was his most public room, accessed via the Lion's Den. Like the Queen's Outer Hall, it was a place where people could wait in the hope of an audience with the king. Depending on your status, life at court could involve a lot of waiting. Those in favour might be invited to attend a meal here at the king's table.

The room is sparsely furnished but handsomely decorated. Above the fireplace is a painting of the royal coat of arms with unicorn supporters. Two friezes run around the walls featuring patterns in the 'grotesque' or 'antique' style that was highly fashionable in the 1530s. The ceiling is coffered – divided into square cells – with painted ribs.

1 The King's Inner Hall.
2 The King's Outer Hall.

1

THE STIRLING HEADS

Perhaps the most famous feature of Stirling Palace's extravagant design is the display of 37 oak roundels, carved in high relief, on the ceiling of the King's Inner Hall.

The ceiling was stripped in 1777, but many of the original carvings survived. A book published in 1817 contains a drawing of each Head by Jane Ferrier (see page 102) and a conjectural illustration by the architect Edward Blore showing all the Heads in place. The surviving originals are too delicate to be replaced on the ceiling, but many of them can be viewed in the Heads Gallery upstairs (see page 35).

1 The ceiling of the King's Inner Hall.
2 One of several Heads depicting Hercules.

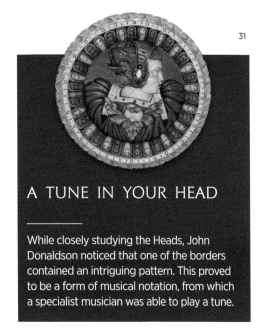

As part of the project to recreate the Palace in its 1540s splendour, a new set of Stirling Heads was commissioned from the Scottish sculptor John Donaldson. These were closely copied from the original Heads or, where they have been lost, from the drawings (see page 102). When complete, these replica Heads were mounted to the repaired ceiling, and colourfully painted in a style appropriate to the original scheme.

The result is an extraordinary field of portraits – some head and shoulders; others full-length – that proclaim the splendour of the Scottish monarch and court. Their subjects range from James V and Mary of Guise to putti (cherubs), mythological figures, emperors, courtiers and a jester.

A TUNE IN YOUR HEAD

While closely studying the Heads, John Donaldson noticed that one of the borders contained an intriguing pattern. This proved to be a form of musical notation, from which a specialist musician was able to play a tune.

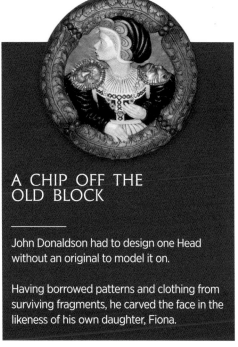

2

A CHIP OFF THE OLD BLOCK

John Donaldson had to design one Head without an original to model it on.

Having borrowed patterns and clothing from surviving fragments, he carved the face in the likeness of his own daughter, Fiona.

WHO'S WHO IN THE STIRLING HEADS

The subjects depicted in the oak roundels fall into various categories, conveying important messages about King James's court.

Kings and Queens: As well as **James V** and **Queen Mary**, the Heads depict a number of royal figures. They include:

- **Madeleine de Valois**, James's late first wife, daughter of François I of France
- **James IV and Margaret Tudor**, James's parents
- **Henry VIII of England**, James's uncle, brother of Margaret Tudor
- **Charles V**, Holy Roman Emperor and King of Spain, an important ally

Roman Emperors: Important signifiers of power at a time when ancient Rome was regarded as a key seat of culture. They include **Titus** and several others.

1 King James I of Scotland.
2 King James IV of Scotland.
3 Madeleine de Valois, first wife of James V.
4 John, Duke of Albany, a former Regent of Scotland.
5 Julius Caesar.
6 Hercules.
7 King Henry VIII of England.
8 A noblewoman at the Scottish court.
9 A performer dressed for a masque, a form of courtly entertainment.

Hercules: The hero of Greek and Roman legend; four different Heads depict famous episodes from his adventures.

The Worthies: These figures – some real; others legendary – embodied Renaissance ideals of virtue and civilisation. Of the nine male and nine female Worthies, seven in total are depicted. They include the Roman general **Julius Caesar** and the crusader knight **Godefroy de Bouillon**, from whom Mary of Guise's family claimed descent.

Courtiers: The people who surrounded the royal couple, reflecting the splendour and sophistication of the court. They include:

- **A masquer** with extravagant headwear of a kind worn by performers of this stylised form of musical drama
- **A poet** with his hand pressed to his chest, suggesting a poetry recital
- **A jester** with provocative stance and mocking face

Putti: Similar to cherubs, these naked children represent divine and romantic love. Many putti are also carved into the Palace's exterior stonework.

WEST GALLERY

The West Gallery was a reception area giving access to both the king's and queen's apartments. Its decorative scheme has not been recreated, allowing visitors to see some of the architectural detail.

In 1603, King James VI became James I of England. He moved with his court to London, returning only once, and Scotland's royal palaces largely fell from use. Over time, they were adapted to other purposes: Stirling became an army garrison.

In the West Gallery, we can see where floors and a staircase were inserted. These adaptations were reversed when the Renaissance finery of the Palace was restored.

1 The Stirling Head representing a court jester.
2 The West Gallery, with evidence of a staircase clearly visible.

3

THE HEADS GALLERY

After leaving the royal apartments, you can view many of the original Stirling Heads and discover more about them in an exhibition occupying the top floor of the Palace.

The original Heads were carved in oak in the 1530s for use on the Palace ceilings. A historic illustration shows them still in place in the King's Inner Hall, where the replicas are now displayed.

Most of the Heads have survived, in full or in part. Three are in the collection of National Museums Scotland in Edinburgh, and can be viewed there.

In the Heads Gallery, the original carvings are grouped by theme, together with insights into the sources and influences behind them.

3 The Heads Gallery on the top floor of the Palace, where visitors can view the original Stirling Heads.

1

THE PRINCE'S TOWER AND WALK

The Heads Gallery leads directly into the Prince's Tower, the west tower of the Forework, which was later incorporated into the Palace.

The Prince's Tower is traditionally believed to have been the nursery and schoolroom of royal children, where the child King James VI spent much of his early life.

James was educated by two tutors: Peter Young and the prominent scholar and historian George Buchanan. Buchanan was a staunch Protestant and one of the chief players in the downfall of James's Catholic mother, Mary Queen of Scots.

Graffiti found scratched into the return of one of the windows is thought to be in James's hand. It reads, 'God made Man and [Wom]an God made Man, James 6.'

Leaving the Prince's Tower, visitors proceed along an elevated walkway known as the Prince's Walk. Above it loom the sculptures decorating the south façade of the Palace.

A naked Devil and other fearsome creatures are among the main figures, perhaps placed here to ward off enemies from the direction of England. Around and above them are smaller figures including men-at-arms.

1 The Prince's Tower and Walk.
2 The graffiti found in a window recess of the Prince's Tower, thought to have been written by a young King James VI.
3 A 19th-century illustration of the Prince's Walk.

EXTERIOR SCULPTURES: EAST AND NORTH WALLS

Symbolic messages are contained in the sculptures that embellish the Palace's walls, overlooking the Outer and Inner Closes.

The main sculptures on the **east façade (Outer Close)** relate to royal power and just government. They are quite badly eroded due to the prevailing weather conditions.

At the far left of the east façade, St Michael is depicted slaying Satan in dragon form.

St Michael is the patron saint of France, and is positioned above the Queen's Bedchamber, giving her extra protection.

Further to the right stands Venus, Roman goddess of love and beauty. Above them are four putti, or cherubs, again symbolising love.

1

The central statue on the **north-east corner** places King James V himself in a prominent position.

The king had himself portrayed with a long beard, perhaps to represent the wisdom of Old Testament prophets. Above him is a crown, and within it, a lion – both symbols of royalty.

On the **north façade (Inner Close)**, the main sculptures are of Classical figures symbolising the prosperity that James's reign was to bring about.

- (Far left) Ganymede, cup-bearer of Zeus, ensuring ample refreshment.

- (Centre left) Venus again, with a peace-loving dove.

- (Centre right) Saturn, overseer of a golden age of peace and plenty.

- (Far right) Abundantia, another Roman goddess representing good fortune.

1 A reconstruction of the Palace's north façade, with the stone carvings complete and brightly painted.
2 Venus, as depicted on the east façade.
3 Ganymede, on the north façade.
4 Saturn, on the north façade.
5 Abundantia, on the north façade.
6 King James V, on the north-east corner.

THE KING'S OLD BUILDING

Above The King's Old Building as it may have looked around 1500.

This much-altered structure was built in the 1490s as the personal residence of King James IV.

It incorporated parts of an earlier residential tower, but was completed and decorated to the fashions of the time.

The building is L-shaped, with a short wing at the north. There was a loggia, or covered walkway, left of the main entrance, and probably a balcony above.

The royal apartment was on the first floor – these principal rooms had large windows overlooking the Inner Close and west to Ben Ledi and the Trossach mountains.

After Stirling Castle fell from royal use, the King's Old Building was adapted for military purposes. It now houses the Regimental Museum of The Argyll and Sutherland Highlanders, who were based at the castle for over 80 years.

MUSEUM OF THE ARGYLL AND SUTHERLAND HIGHLANDERS

The Argyll and Sutherland Highlanders have longstanding connections with Stirling Castle.

The 98th (later 91st) Argyllshire Highlanders were raised here in 1794. They amalgamated with the 93rd Sutherland Highlanders in 1881 to form The Argyll and Sutherland Highlanders (Princess Louise's). They had their headquarters here from 1873 until 2006. The Regimental Museum is housed in The King's Old Building.

The Regiment's roots can be traced to the Stirlingshire Militia, raised at the Castle in 1639, which fought under the Royalist Marquess of Montrose in the Covenanting Wars. A silver centrepiece of Montrose stands in the first gallery, where you enter the museum.

Below The first muster of the 98th Argyllshire Highlanders below Stirling Castle in 1794.

MUSEUM OF THE ARGYLL AND SUTHERLAND HIGHLANDERS (CONT.)

The museum's galleries occupy three floors. Each adopts a different theme.

Service to the Crown

This gallery provides an orientation to the Regiment's history, 1794–2006. It recognises the Royal connections of a regiment that carries the name of Queen Victoria's daughter, HRH The Princess Louise, Duchess of Argyll.

❶ Photographs of HRH The Princess Elizabeth (later HM The Queen) during her first visit to Stirling as Colonel-in-Chief of the Regiment in 1947.

❷ Two of the medals of Lieutenant McBean, who fought at Lucknow, India, in 1857.

Our Argyll Family

This gallery focuses on The Argylls' tradition of caring for and remembering their own, together with the associations it enjoys with sister regiments.

Our Scottish Roots

Exploring the links between the Regiment's soldiers and the communities from which they came, this gallery highlights the impact of the Highland Clearances, the industrialisation of Clydeside, the substantial role played by the Territorial Force and the new opportunities that arose for women in the First World War.

3 The silver statuette of the Regimental Mascot, a pony named Cruachan II. It was displayed in the Warrant Officers' and Sergeants' Mess.

4 Women factory workers during the First World War.

Prisoners of War

At times, soldiers of The Argylls have been captured and become prisoners of war, sometimes in barbaric conditions. This gallery explores the challenges of captivity and highlights some brave escapes.

Staying Alive

This gallery explores the impact of weapons and disease on the fragile human body, and demonstrates how some good comes from the evil of war as it has driven forward the boundaries of medicine.

5 Instruments of William Monro, Surgeon to both the 91st and 93rd Regiments in the 1840s–60s, offer an insight into what was then pioneering treatment.

MUSEUM OF THE ARGYLL AND SUTHERLAND HIGHLANDERS (CONT.)

Further galleries cover other aspects of the Regiment's story.

Spirit of the Argylls

This gallery reveals the pastoral life of the Regiment. With special focus on the 'Jocks' and their families, it touches on sport, music, religion and daily life.

❶ The bagpipes of Pipe Major William Lawrie, 8th (The Argyllshire) Battalion, together with the score of his composition 'The Battle of the Somme'.

Fearless in Battle

A gallery celebrating the qualities of the Regiment's soldiers in conflicts spanning 220 years, including audio-visual vignettes of several key campaigns.

❷ Robert Gibb's painting *The Thin Red Line*, depicts the 93rd Sutherland Highlanders repulsing an attack by Russian cavalry at the Battle of Balaklava in 1854.

Our Legacy Lives On

This gallery is dedicated to the Regiment's successors since 2006, The Royal Regiment of Scotland (SCOTS). The film *Perspectives of War* explains the soldiers' role and that played by the government and the media.

3 The equipment worn by Captain Niall Archibald of 5 SCOTS in Afghanistan in 2010–11.

The Officers' Mess

The Officers' Mess was the home to junior officers, where visitors were warmly received. The table is set for a Regimental Guest Night.

Laid to Rest

This gallery houses the Last Stand of 1st Battalion's Colours. In the past they were carried into battle and served as the rallying point for the troops. They are central to a Regiment's identity.

4 The Regimental Colour, presented by HM The Queen in 1996, and embroidered with some of the Regiment's Battle Honours: the conflicts where it has served with distinction.

Colours Room

Further stands of Colours are displayed in this final gallery, including those carried at Balaklava in 1854. Around the walls is a collection of paintings of The Argylls in action along with the 1st Battalion's spectacular silver centre-piece.

5 Peter Archer's painting *Fighting Spirit* depicts soldiers of the 2nd Battalion climbing from an enemy trench to advance at the Somme in 1916.

THE GREAT HALL

The Great Hall is one of the finest and largest late-medieval buildings in Scotland. It was built around 1500–1503.

This was perhaps King James IV's most ambitious expression of power and prestige, an imposing venue for banquets and state occasions. It was also used by castle servants as a dining room and dormitory.

The main entrance, from the Inner Close, opens into a servery for banquets. In the principal space, the focus is on the dais, or raised section, where the king, queen and their most honoured guests would have sat, lit by enormous bay windows. Elsewhere, the windows are smaller, set high in the walls. The restored hammerbeam ceiling incorporates about 4,000 handmade oak pegs. There are five fireplaces to heat this enormous space.

As well as the main hall, there are storage cellars, a musicians' gallery above the servery and an external walkway around the parapet. When the Palace was built in 1538, a bridge was constructed, connecting it to the Great Hall.

Right The Great Hall interior, laid out for a formal dinner.

Royal use of Stirling Castle declined sharply after James VI became King of England in 1603, and over time the Great Hall was adapted for military use. In the 1790s, it was subdivided into barrack rooms over three floors. The hammerbeam roof, formed from a complex structure of timber beams, was destroyed at that time, but has since been reconstructed.

By the 1850s, the building's shortcomings as military accommodation were notorious; however, it was not until 1964 that work began to restore it to its present state. The work was completed in 1999.

REIGN AND SHINE

The building is harled with an authentic lime render known as 'King's Gold'. Pale yellow in sunny conditions, it takes on a deep golden glow in wet weather.

1

THE CHAPEL ROYAL

This expansive chapel was commissioned by James VI in 1594, for the baptism of his firstborn son, Prince Henry. It was Stirling's last royal building.

The chapel occupies most of the north side of the Inner Close. It replaced an earlier chapel royal, which stood on roughly the same site – its layout is outlined in the cobbles.

The new building was designed for Protestant rather than Catholic worship, with a pulpit near the centre. The architecture may have drawn inspiration from the Danish palace of Kronborg (Elsinore), where James's proxy marriage to Queen Anna was held in 1589.

The interior decorative scheme dates from 1594. It includes the cypher I6R (for Iacobus Rex 6: King James VI), among scrolls and other motifs, and a *trompe l'oeil* (false)

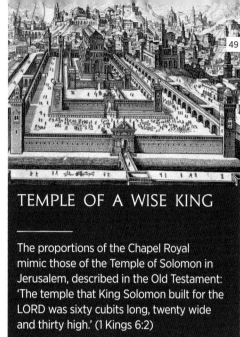

TEMPLE OF A WISE KING

The proportions of the Chapel Royal mimic those of the Temple of Solomon in Jerusalem, described in the Old Testament: 'The temple that King Solomon built for the LORD was sixty cubits long, twenty wide and thirty high.' (1 Kings 6:2)

window in the east gable. The paintwork was refreshed in 1628 in anticipation of Charles I's Scottish coronation, and again in 1951. There are also traces of paint on the exterior, which may also have been lavishly decorated.

Henry's baptism in the chapel was the central event of an extravagant celebration, at which many of Europe's major powers were represented. A vivid eyewitness account of the ceremony survives (see pages 98–99).

1 The Chapel Royal, one of the last royal buildings in Scotland.
2 A detail of the interior decoration scheme, originally painted in 1594.

In 1603, James became King of England and Ireland, while remaining King of Scots. Prince Henry proved a vigorous and dynamic heir, but never inherited the triple throne. He died aged 18 in 1612, so it was his younger brother Charles who succeeded James in 1625.

THE DOUGLAS GARDEN AND THE WALL-WALKS

This secluded enclosure occupies the highest part of Castle Rock, and was probably the main focus of the earliest fortifications, though no visible trace survives. It has been a garden since the 1500s.

The name is said to derive from William, 8th Earl of Douglas, who was stabbed and killed in February 1452 during a brawl with King James II, then flung from a window.

According to tradition, these dramatic events took place in the King's Old Building, which was not built until half a century later. However, James II's royal lodging was probably in this approximate location.

Elevated walkways, or wall-walks, run along the inside of the curtain wall in the Douglas Garden and elsewhere on the outer faces of the castle. This one continues uninterrupted to the Outer Close.

The wall-walks were created in the early 1700s, when Theodore Dury refortified the castle, though they may have replaced an earlier system of wall-walks.

They allowed sentries to patrol the castle perimeter from a position of safety, giving them a clear view over the surrounding countryside. Visitors can use them for the same purpose.

WOMEN AND THE WAR EFFORT

The Auxiliary Territorial Service was a women's unit of the armed forces formed in 1938. Its members carried out communications, cooking, driving, anti-aircraft, and other essential roles during the Second World War. The ATS's base at Stirling Castle was in the Douglas Garden. The large brick building, now demolished, had a kitchen, a dining room, sitting rooms, and an office.

1 The Douglas Garden, overlooked by the King's Old Building.
2 Steps leading up to the wall-walk in the Douglas Garden.

1

THE GREAT KITCHENS

Adjacent to the North Gate are large kitchens where banquets could be prepared for many guests.

They were built in the early 1500s to serve the new Great Hall. In 1689, they were abandoned and filled in when the Grand Battery was built in their place. They were rediscovered in 1921, during the earliest archaeological investigations at the castle.

They have now been recreated to show castle staff hard at work preparing food.

MAKING MONEY

There is a tradition that the North Gate kitchens were once used as a mint. We know that coins were struck in Stirling, but there is no evidence to support this as the venue.

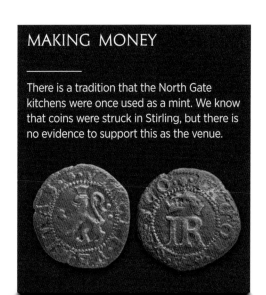

THE NORTH GATE

Connecting the Outer Close to the Nether Bailey, the North Gate was built in 1381. It is the oldest surviving structure in the castle, though buildings existed here long before that.

The North Gate was never a main entrance into the castle, but allowed traffic to and from the Nether Bailey, which linked to the outside via two small posterns (rear gateways). Its late-medieval fabric includes the archway at the lower end, which was once defended by a portcullis.

The upper floors of the North Gate were adapted around 1511–12 to create additional kitchens for the Great Hall: two substantial rooms, each with a large hearth. Dishes were served via a lobby between this building and the hall.

In the early 1700s these rooms became a brewhouse to make ale for the castle garrison.

1 A costumed interpreter helps prepare vegetables in the Great Kitchens.
2 The North Gate (left of centre), with the access to the Great Kitchens at the right.

1

THE NETHER BAILEY

STITCHES IN TIME

The Tapestry Studio was purpose-built in 2003–4, during the 13-year project to weave the Hunt of the Unicorn tapestries. Three of the seven tapestries were woven here. After the completion of the final tapestry in 2013, the studio was reconfigured as an exhibition space, giving insights into the development and completion of this unique project, the techniques used and the interpretation of the Unicorn narrative.

The Nether Bailey was probably always secondary to the Inner and Outer Closes, connecting to them via the North Gate.

The rocky terrain of this enclosure meant that it was not suitable for large buildings. It was used throughout the castle's history for secondary functions such as guard rooms, workshops and store-rooms, stables, kennels and carefully reinforced magazines for storage of gunpowder.

The wall-walk around the Nether Bailey is accessible to visitors, allowing views to the north and east. It incorporates two posterns or rear entrances, which originally allowed access to lower ground via Castle Rock, though they were later blocked.

At the far end of the Nether Bailey is the Tapestry Exhibition, in the studio where some of the Stirling Tapestries were woven.

1 The Nether Bailey, with the Tapestry Studio at the far end.
2 Weaver Mieko Konaka at work in the studio.

1

THE RECREATIONAL LANDSCAPE

The royal residents of Stirling did not confine themselves to the castle, but engaged in hunting, horse riding, falconry, jousting, archery and other pursuits in the surrounding countryside. (See page 58.)

The crown also owned pasture grounds for cattle and horses, and adjoining fields to grow crops for the royal household and its livestock.

In the Renaissance, carefully crafted gardens were prized, providing colourful and fragrant surroundings for the royal court. Extensive gardens were laid out on the slopes and plains around the castle, incorporating orchards, fish ponds and a loch with swans and herons.

James IV was himself a keen gardener: he had a thousand trees planted here in 1497. Mary of Guise brought plum and pear trees here from France in 1538.

The most obvious survivals are the King's and Queen's Knots, which lie below the castle to the west. These geometrical earthworks probably date from 1625–36, when a gardener named Watt was employed, and granted significant funds to engage workmen for the 'plotting and reforming of his majesty's gairdins'.

1 *Stirling in the Time of the Stuarts*, painted by Johannes Vosterman in the 1670s.
2 Hawking was a popular pursuit for wealthy people in medieval Scotland.

2

herue de meriadet / comba
tirent es lices trois chlze
escochois et en partirent
a leur tresgrant honneur

coce
frou
gue
de l
de la
arm
tou
tes
esto
laca
mes
des
Issi
ma
nes
te d
tou
gas
et
et d

ROYAL SPORT

Hunting, hawking and tournaments were important elite pursuits, and Stirling's royal residents took full advantage of the surrounding parks and grounds.

The earliest reference to a royal forest, or hunting reserve, at Stirling is from 1143, during the reign of David I. Stirling's Old Park and New Park, where deer were enclosed, were created in the later 1100s and mid-1200s, to the south and west of the castle.

James IV renovated the Old Park in the late 1400s and early 1500s. He had deer transported there from Falkland, in litters drawn by horses. James also took a keen interest in hawking. Dedicated staff called falconers included Andrew Doull, who looked after the king's hawks at Stirling and other royal residences.

As well as hunting, Stirling was a favourite location for tournaments. In his romance, *Méliador*, written in the 1380s, chronicler Jean Froissart referred to Stirling as 'a castle in Scotland strong and beautiful ... where one goes to tourney'.

In 1449 a tournament was held at Stirling Castle, shortly before Mary of Guelders arrived from Burgundy to marry James II. The Scottish combatants were the Earl of Douglas's brother, James, James Douglas of Ralston, and John Ross of Hawkhead, reportedly accompanied by 4–5,000 men. The Burgundian challengers were Hervé de Meriadec, Simon de Lalaing, and Simon's nephew, Jacques: the latter an internationally famous tourneyer.

The two teams fought on foot using lances, axes, swords, and daggers. The tournament was conducted *à outrance*, meaning that unblunted weapons were used, and there was a real risk of serious injury or death. The Burgundians were on the point of winning when the king called a halt to the fighting, preserving the Scots' lives.

2

1 An illustration from *The Book of the Deeds of Jacques de Lalaing* depicts the 1449 tournament in Stirling.
2 King James IV depicted with a falcon.

MAR'S WARK

Nearby lies a building of the 1500s with close connections to the castle. Mar's Wark (meaning 'work') was built as a residence for the powerful Earl and Countess of Mar.

It was begun sometime after the Reformation of 1560, when Cambuskenneth Abbey, Dryburgh Abbey and Inchmahome Priory were dissolved and the earl obtained their wealth. However, it was described as 'empty and not completed' in 1571.

Mar died a year later, so he may never have occupied it. What survives is a façade – its gateway flanked by two towers – with scant remains behind.

This was a very elegant and fashionable building. Many carved stone details survive, including the earl and countess's coats of arms and an inscription:

*'I pray all lookers on this lodging
With gentle eye to give their judging.'*

WHO WERE THE MARS?

John Erskine, Earl of Mar, *below*, and Annabella Murray, Countess of Mar, were prominent figures at the court of Mary Queen of Scots. They became custodians of royal children, including James VI and his son Prince Henry. The child King James was kept at Stirling by the Mars for over a decade, without ever leaving the castle.

In 1571, Mar was elected Regent, governing Scotland on behalf of James, until his death at Stirling Castle a year later. Countess Annabella continued in her role. Her care of the young Prince Henry brought her into conflict with his mother Queen Anna, who wanted to keep her children with her rather than in separate households. 'Old Lady Mar' was asked to leave Stirling Castle when Anna planned to visit her son in April 1595. She died in 1603.

JOAN ALONE

A carved figure in a burial shroud is said to represent Joan of Arc, martyred heroine of the Hundred Years' War. Her French name Jeanne d'Arc was rendered locally as 'Jeannie Dark'.

THE HISTORY OF STIRLING CASTLE

Situated at the centre of Scotland, both geographically and symbolically, Stirling Castle has for many centuries played a pivotal role in our history.

Over the years it was a valuable prize to be won in war, a family home and royal nursery for kings and queens, an important military base, and now a popular heritage attraction. Often, the castle performed multiple functions at the same time.

During the Wars of Independence, Stirling was the target of numerous sieges. One of these led to the Battle of Bannockburn in 1314, at which Robert I reinforced his kingship of Scotland.

Stirling Castle was favoured by the Stewart dynasty, particularly in the 1400s and 1500s. They spent their formative years here, protected from harm by their strategic situation high up on the Castle Rock. As a centre of power, it was the location of royal baptisms and coronations.

1 A set of toy soldiers and horses, discovered under the floorboards of the Palace in 2009. They probably date from the mid-1800s.

1

Since the 1700s, the castle has been a subject of historical and artistic curiosity. Recognised as a place that can tell us, through physical evidence, about the lives and events of the past, it continues to fascinate visitors to this day.

'Here Stewarts once in glory reign'd,
And laws for Scotland's weal ordain'd,
But now unroof'd their palace stands,
Their sceptre fallen to other hands.'

– Robert Burns (1787)

TIMELINE
1297–1561

1297
—

Sir William Wallace and Sir Andrew Murray, *right*, lead an army that massacres English forces at Stirling Bridge, within sight of the castle.

1371
—

Robert II, *left*, becomes the first in a long line of Stewart monarchs. He orders rebuilding at Stirling Castle, including the North Gate, now the castle's oldest structure.

1452
—

James II, *left*, kills William, Earl of Douglas during a brawl at Stirling Castle.

1538
—

James V, *right*, commissions the hugely ambitious Royal Palace as a residence for himself and Queen Mary of Guise.

1543
—

Mary Queen of Scots is crowned, *right*, at Stirling, at nine months the youngest of Scotland's many child monarchs.

1314
—

Robert I (the Bruce), *left*, defeats Edward II of England's army at Bannockburn, near Stirling, in a celebrated victory.

1336
—

Edward III of England's forces seize and refortify Stirling Castle, which they hold until its recapture by the Scots in 1342.

1503
—

The Great Hall, *left*, is completed, Scotland's grandest secular building, and the culmination of James IV's architectural additions at Stirling.

1503
—

Margaret Tudor, *left*, marries James IV, setting the seal on a 'Treaty of Perpetual Peace' between Scotland and England. James commissions a residential suite for her at Stirling.

1554
—

Mary of Guise, *right*, becomes regent, governing Scotland on behalf of her 11-year-old daughter, now living in France.

1561
—

Mary Queen of Scots, *right*, returns to reign, following the deaths of her mother, Mary of Guise and her husband, François II of France.

TIMELINE 1566–1873

1566
—

Prince James, *right*, is baptised at Stirling Castle. A year later, Queen Mary is forced to abdicate and James becomes another child monarch.

1594
—

Prince Henry, *right*, is born, heir to the throne. James VI has the Chapel Royal built as the venue for his son's baptism. Henry will die at 18, without becoming king.

1645
—

James Graham, Marquess of Montrose, *left*, leads a Royalist army against Covenanting forces at Inverlochy and Kilsyth. His troops include the Stirlingshire Militia, raised at the castle in 1639.

1651
—

General George Monck, *left*, captures Stirling Castle for the English parliamentary army, following the Scottish coronation of Charles II.

1794
—

The 98th (later 91st) Argyllshire Highlanders , *left*, are raised on the King's Knot below the castle, one of two regiments that will become the Argyll and Sutherland Highlanders.

1817
—

Jane Ferrier, *left*, publishes a book of her drawings of Stirling Castle, which includes a detailed illustration of each Stirling Head.

1625

Charles I, *right*, succeeds his father James VI of Scotland and I of England. Stirling Castle is refurbished in anticipation of a Scottish coronation, which does not take place until 1633.

1708–14
—
Captain Theodore Dury redevelops the military defences of Stirling Castle, including the present Outer Defences, *left*.

1715
—
James Erskine, 6th Earl of Mar, *left*, governor of Stirling Castle, launches a Jacobite Rising, intending to install Prince James Francis Edward Stuart on the throne.

1842
—
Queen Victoria, *left*, visits Stirling Castle, including 'the room in which James IInd killed Douglas, & the window out of which he was thrown'.

1873
—
The 91st Argyllshire Highlanders, *left*, establish a depot at Stirling Castle, from which they deploy across the world. The castle continues in this role until 1964.

CASTLE ROCK

Stirling Castle sits in a physically prominent position, overlooking the Forth valley from a volcanic rock millions of years old.

The rock was formed by glaciers during the Ice Age, with almost vertical slopes leading up to the summit except for a gentler ascent from the south-east, along which the burgh later developed. This position overlooks a strategically important part of central Scotland, allowing its inhabitants to dominate travel and communication between east and west and between Highlands and Lowlands.

It is unknown when people first inhabited and fortified the Castle Rock, but it may have been as early as the Iron Age. It would have been difficult to build on top of it, requiring levelling and drainage. This meant that the expansion of the castle's buildings and fortifications would have occurred over several centuries.

The land around the River Forth, which winds its way through the valley close to the castle, is surrounded by land which can be extremely wet and boggy. These conditions were to have significant consequences for the castle during the Wars of Independence, at the Battles of Stirling Bridge and Bannockburn.

Above A view of the castle from the north-west.

NAMED AND SHAMED

In a Gaelic tradition the Devil was in charge of building the castle. He agreed that the laird did not need to pay if he could find out the Devil's name before the castle was completed. The laird heard workers referring to Thomas Jock, forcing the Devil to leave without his wages: 'Stirling Castle completed and poor Thomas Jock destitute!'

Above The Devil, as depicted in a sculpture on the south face of the Palace.

THE MEDIEVAL ROYAL CASTLE

The earliest known documentary reference to Stirling Castle records that Alexander I (reigned 1107–24) dedicated the castle chapel to St Michael.

Religion was to play an important part in the establishment of royal power at Stirling. David I founded Cambuskenneth Abbey, a mile to the east, in the 1140s. David was remembered by chronicler Andrew Wyntoun as a pious king who 'illumined his lands with kirks and abbeys'.

The abbey was maintained financially by the properties, farms, fisheries, and other landed resources granted to it by David, his daughter-in-law, Ada de Warenne, and other wealthy patrons. Its Augustinian clergy were to play a significant role in the spiritual life of royal residents over the next few centuries.

The castle was designed as a symbol of royal power, and was surrounded by extensive estates to provide food for the royal family and their large household. The earliest structures of the castle were probably made of wood, aside from the stone chapel. They included comfortable accommodation for the king and queen.

In 1173, William I supported a rebellion against Henry II of England, led by Henry's wife, Eleanor of Aquitaine, and their sons. William was captured in 1174 and held to ransom. He was forced to sign Stirling and other castles over to Henry – though the transfer of ownership was never fully enacted. William died at Stirling in 1214.

By the late 1200s, when 'Ricardus cementarius' – Richard the mason – is recorded working here, the buildings were increasingly built in stone. Stirling's position as an important royal centre was being solidified.

Above A visit by King David I with his son Earl Henry and daughter-in-law Ada de Warenne to oversee the building of Cambuskenneth Abbey. Stirling Castle is visible on the horizon.

2

THE WARS OF INDEPENDENCE: EARLY YEARS

The deaths of Alexander III in 1286 and his granddaughter, Margaret of Norway, in 1290 left Scotland without a monarch.

Edward I of England was invited to arbitrate and decided that John Balliol, Lord of Galloway had the best claim to the throne. However, Edward was at war with France and, when Scotland formed an alliance with the French, he saw this as betrayal. He removed Balliol as king and invaded Scotland in March 1296.

In 1297 an army led by William Wallace and Andrew Murray roundly defeated English forces at nearby Stirling Bridge. The Scots trapped the English as the latter crossed the narrow bridge. The English leader Hugh Cressingham was killed, and his skin used to make a sword belt for Wallace. Murray also received fatal wounds. The following year, at Falkirk, the English regained the upper hand when they defeated Wallace. In 1305 Wallace was captured and brutally executed.

By 1304 Edward was gathering support from Scottish nobles, including Robert Bruce, Earl of Carrick. Bruce was present at Edward's three-month-long siege of Stirling, where an audience including Edward's queen, Margaret of France, watched siege engines bombard the castle with 'Greek fire'.

The surviving garrison of 25 surrendered but Edward did not release them until his great trebuchet, the War Wolf, had destroyed a wall of the castle. Edward's knights celebrated their victory by jousting before their departure.

During the siege, Bruce met Bishop William Lamberton of St Andrews at nearby Cambuskenneth Abbey. There they promised to support each other above all others, suggesting that Bruce was already planning to become king himself.

1 An artist's impression of the siege of 1304, when Edward I deployed his siege engine War Wolf against Stirling Castle.
2 Edward I of England, as depicted on a manuscript of the 1500s.

BRUCE AND BANNOCKBURN

Robert I became king in 1306 and began a long and bloody campaign to assert his right to reign, free from English interference.

In spring 1314, his forces besieged Stirling Castle, the defenders agreeing to surrender if they were not relieved by 24 June.

Stirling's constable, Philip Mowbray reported to King Edward II that 'horses will find it difficult to enter' the wet terrain around the Bannock burn, two miles south of the castle. Despite this, Edward's army met Bruce's there and skirmished on 23 June. In the New Park, Robert triumphed in one-on-one combat with English knight Henry de Bohun, killing him with an axe.

The next day, the Scots surprised the English by emerging from Balquidderock Wood. Without enough ground to deploy their cavalry, the English and their horses fell back into the steep, deep Bannock burn and were massacred. Edward II fled to the castle, having lost his shield, several high-status hostages, and the lives of thousands of soldiers, but Mowbray refused him entry and Edward escaped to England.

In November 1314 Robert held a parliament at Cambuskenneth Abbey. Scottish nobles who had not come into his allegiance were forfeited of their lands and titles, to be redistributed to his loyal supporters.

Victory allowed Robert to demand the return of his wife, Elizabeth de Burgh, his daughter, Marjorie, and his sisters, Christina and Mary, from imprisonment in England. The king could now look to producing a legitimate male heir with Elizabeth. First, though, he had Stirling Castle reduced to the ground so that the English could not occupy it again.

THE FINAL BLOW

'Nother hat na helm mycht stynt
The hevy dusche that he him gave
That ner the heid till the harnyss clave'

'Neither hat nor helmet could withstand
The heavy blow [Bruce] gave to [Bohun]
That split his head to the brains'

– John Barbour, *The Bruce,* 1375

1 The Battle of Bannockburn, as depicted in a manuscript of the 1400s.
2 Edward II, from a manuscript of about 1320.

STIRLING CASTLE UNDER SIEGE

Stirling Castle was a valuable prize for both sides in the Wars of Independence. It changed hands numerous times: in 1296, 1297, 1298, 1299, 1304, 1314, 1336, and 1342.

Those who took the castle could punish their enemies harshly. A townswoman, Eva, had supplied the English garrison with victuals. When the Scots regained the castle in 1299, they imprisoned Eva for ten weeks then expelled her from Scotland. She lost her house and three acres of land.

Laying siege, too, was dangerous. When William Keith was climbing the castle wall in 1337, the defenders threw down a stone which caused him to fall, 'And stekyd hym on his awyn spere: And off that wounde sone deyde he.'

Nearby Cambuskenneth Abbey was also affected 'by the wars which had for a very long time raged in those parts, and by the conduct of certain sons of iniquity, who had seized and carried off the chalices, books and the rest of the ornaments of the altar, and other goods belonging to the abbey'.

1 A medieval arrowhead found at Stirling Castle.
2 A trebuchet, or catapult, one of the most feared siege weapons before the advent of cannon.
3 A row of four armed stone guards line the Palace roof above the Prince's Walk. They are facing south towards England, then seen as a military threat.

GOING BALLISTIC

Around 1340 Stirling saw the earliest known use of cannons in Scotland, according to chronicler Jean Froissart, who wrote that the Scots used them against the castle.

AFTER BANNOCKBURN

1

Despite victory at Bannockburn, the birth of Bruce's heir, David, and the conclusion of a peace treaty in 1328, the Wars of Independence were not over.

Between 1332 and 1357, supporters of David II and Edward Balliol continued to fight for control of Scotland. Stirling Castle was finally won by the Scots, led by the future Robert II, in 1342.

Having failed to produce children with his first two wives, David II installed his mistress, Agnes Dunbar, in the castle in 1370. However, the pair did not marry, and David never produced an heir.

1 The seal of Edward Balliol, son of King John Balliol, who briefly seized the throne in 1332.
2 King Edward III of England, who supported Edward Balliol's bid for the Scottish throne.

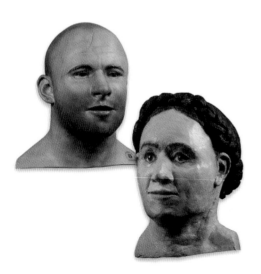

CASUALTIES OF WAR

The effects of the Wars of Independence are still evident today. Several people who suffered violent deaths around that time have been found buried at the castle. One woman, aged 26 to 45, had sustained head injuries from a war hammer or poleaxe, perhaps during a siege. Their remains were discovered between the Palace and the King's Old Building, previously the site of a chapel.

Left Reconstructed heads of a knight and a woman found buried under the castle's old chapel.

JAMES I AND JOAN BEAUFORT

The absence of the young king in the early 1400s meant that the country was governed by the powerful Duke of Albany.

James I became king in 1406 at the age of 11. However, the month before his accession he was captured by pirates and held prisoner in England for the next 18 years.

Authority in Scotland was exercised by his uncle, Robert, 1st Duke of Albany. Albany died at Stirling Castle in 1420. He was remembered as 'a mirror in which true justice has shone, and whatever the world admires in a prince'.

Robert's son, Murdoch, 2nd Duke of Albany, became the new governor of Scotland. He was, in contrast, 'too slack in the exercise of this office', and his sons were 'persons devoting themselves to what they liked and not to what was lawful'.

James I returned to Scotland and in 1425 he had Murdoch and his family arrested. Murdoch, his sons, Walter and Alexander, and his father-in-law, Duncan, Earl of Lennox, were beheaded, while his wife, Isabella Stewart, was imprisoned for many years.

As part of the agreement for James's release, he married Joan Beaufort, an English lady. Although this was a political arrangement, the couple were close. In his great literary work, *The Kingis Quair*, James wrote of Joan that,

'In hir was youth, beautee with humble aport [bearing],
Bountee, richesse and wommanly facture [feminine form]–
God better wote [knows] than my pen can report –
Wisdome, largesse, estate and connyng [intelligence] sure.
In every poynt so guydit hir mesure,
In word, in dede, in schap, in contenance,
That Nature myght no more hir childe avance [improve].'

After struggling for years to establish his authority over his nobles, James was assassinated in 1437, but a wounded Joan managed to escape.

Right James I and Joan Beaufort, as depicted in the Forman Armorial, a manuscript produced around 1562.

IAMES THE FIRST IN MARIAGE DID GET
NANS DOCHTER TO YE ERLL OF SOMERSET
ANE INGLIS LORD OF HONOVR AND RENOVN
THIS IAMES THE FIRST SCHORT QVHILE
POSSEST THE CROVN

JAMES II AND MARY OF GUELDERS

After her husband's death, Queen Joan took command and had James I's killers punished, but she was soon replaced as regent.

In 1439 Joan and her new husband, James Stewart of Lorne, took her son, James II, to Stirling. Alexander Livingston, captain of Stirling Castle, imprisoned them and Joan was forced to give custody of her son to him.

In 1449, when James was 18, he started his own family by marrying Mary of Guelders, great-niece of the Duke of Burgundy. As part of her dower – to be her property after the king's death – Mary was granted Stirling Castle, and this tradition was followed for subsequent queens consort. At Stirling Mary gave premature birth to her first child, who died six hours later.

In 1452 James dined at the castle with William, 8th Earl of Douglas. The king asked Douglas to break his alliance with the earls of Crawford and Ross, which Douglas refused to do, James calling him a 'fals tratour'. The king stabbed Douglas multiple times before one of his men 'strak out his branes' with a poleaxe.

POOR THINGS

Mary of Guelders regularly gave charity to six paupers who lived outside the castle gate between 1460 and 1463. She gave them money, coal, and grain in a highly visible symbol of her piety and generosity.

JAMES III AND MARGARET OF DENMARK

James II was killed when one of his own cannon exploded in 1460, and was succeeded by his young son James III.

The new king lived mostly in Edinburgh, but he did pay for repairs at Stirling Castle. He also founded the old Chapel Royal in around 1470, and provided it with vestments, bread for the Mass, incense, and donations of money.

James and Margaret of Denmark's three sons, including the future James IV, grew up at Stirling in their mother's custody. The couple lived apart for the last six years of Margaret's life. After giving birth to three sons, Margaret perhaps considered her duty fulfilled. James is said to have respected his wife's piety, and after her death petitioned the pope for her to be canonised as a saint.

To teach her son, James, to be a courteous ruler, Margaret is said to have had him serve her at table, cutting her meat and giving her water to wash her hands. In 1486, as she lay dying at Stirling, she advised James to always do good, 'because nothing achieved by violence, be certain, can endure'.

Two years later, Prince James became the teenage figurehead of a rebellion against his unpopular father. This led to the king's death during or after the Battle of Sauchieburn, at or near the site of Bannockburn.

This page James III and Margaret of Denmark as depicted by the Flemish artist Hugo van der Goes for an altarpiece at Trinity College Kirk in Edinburgh, late 1470s. The future James IV is seen kneeling behind his father.

James the fourt
Began His Rawne
1489 He maried
Margaret eldest dochter
of Henry the Sebinth

JAMES IV AND MARGARET TUDOR

After being implicated in his father's killing, James IV did lifelong penance and was a devoutly religious king.

In 1488, he attended his father's burial at Cambuskenneth Abbey, where he had a marble tomb constructed for his parents. 'Deploiring and lamenting the deid of his father' to George Vaus, dean of the Chapel Royal at Stirling, for the rest of his life James wore an iron belt underneath his clothes as penance.

The castle once again became a family home as the nursery for James's children by Marion Boyd, Margaret Drummond, Janet Kennedy, and Isabel Stewart. James's mistresses had prominent positions, living at Stirling Castle for a time, and were provided with lands and incomes.

In 1503 James married the 13-year-old English princess, Margaret Tudor. Stirling's Great Hall, with large windows at the dais end, may have been designed as a compliment to Margaret's heritage, as this arrangement was common in England.

By now James's own residence the King's Old Building was complete, and he probably also commissioned a range of buildings for Margaret on the site now occupied by the west side of the Palace.

James and Margaret's first child, James – an older brother of the future James V – was baptised at Stirling in 1507, lavishly dressed in cloth of gold and ermine. Unfortunately, he died there the following year, and James V was the only child of theirs to survive infancy.

Prince James was barely a year old in 1513 when his father invaded the north of England. When King James's army met an English force at Flodden in Northumberland, thousands of Scots were killed, including the king and many of his nobles.

1 James IV and Margaret Tudor, as depicted in the Seton Armorial of 1591.
2 A Victorian stone chest marking the burial place of James IV's parents at Cambuskenneth Abbey.

SCOTLAND'S RENAISSANCE: ARTS, LITERATURE AND SCIENCE

During the Renaissance of the 1400s and 1500s, the monarchs of Scotland cultivated arts and culture. Under James IV, much of the castle as we see it today was created, including the Great Hall, larger than that of Edinburgh Castle, the King's Old Building, and the great towered Forework.

James staffed the Chapel Royal with a dean, dignitaries, canons, and choristers, all skilled in music. Robert Carver was probably based at the Chapel Royal when he composed some of the finest polyphonic liturgical music to survive from Renaissance Scotland.

Also based at Stirling was alchemist John Damian, who tried to make *quinta essencia* – the fifth element. Damian was given gold, silver, mercury, other ingredients, and a team of assistants to make the magical substance, but never succeeded. His contemporary, the poet William Dunbar, mocked Damian by imagining him attempting to fly using bird feathers but falling 'in a myre vp to the ene [eyes]'.

1 One of the Stirling Heads depicts a poet reciting his work.
2 An artist's impression of William Dunbar, a prominent poet at the court of James IV.

James also had a great interest in literature, music, and science. Although he could speak seven other languages including Gaelic, his court was a centre for authors and poets writing in Scots, including Walter Kennedy, uncle of James's mistress, Janet.

This flourishing of Scots continued into the reign of James V, when David Lyndsay wrote works about politics and morality.

The Scottish Renaissance court was populated, wrote Dunbar, by 'kirkmen, courtmen and craftsmen fine' – though there were also, at Stirling, those who 'far can multiplie in folie'.

Stirling Castle in this era was furnished with the finest items. Some were made in Scotland, while others were provided by international merchants, such as the royal tapestry collection, imported from Flanders and France.

Below A modern performance of *A Satire of the Three Estates*, written by Sir David Lyndsay, a herald at the court of James V.

1

JAMES V AND MARY OF GUISE

James IV died in battle in 1513, leaving his one-year-old son James V as monarch. The new king grew up with ambitions to assert himself as a powerful ruler of the European Renaissance.

By James IV's will, his widow, Margaret Tudor, was to be regent for the young James V as long as she didn't remarry.

However, in 1514 she married Archibald Douglas, 6th Earl of Angus and was replaced as regent by John Stewart, 2nd Duke of Albany. Albany led an army to Stirling and took custody of James and his brother, Alexander.

In the 1520s Margaret and Albany ruled jointly, but in 1527–8, Margaret divorced Douglas and married her treasurer, Henry Stewart without James's permission. James agreed to accept the marriage in exchange for Stirling, which had been part of Margaret's dower.

James V commissioned the spectacular palace block to be his own family home. His first bride, Madeleine of Valois, never made it to Stirling. Her successor, Mary of Guise, asked her mother, Antoinette de Bourbon, to send French masons to work at the castle, adding to the improvements already begun by James.

REX ✝ SCOTORVM

M·R

James and Mary's second son, Robert, was born at Stirling, but he and his elder brother, James, both died in infancy. James V's successor, when he died in 1542, was to be his newborn daughter, Mary.

1 The 'impaled', or combined, coats of arms of James V and Mary of Guise.
2 Wedding portrait of James and Mary.

LAW UNTO THEMSELVES

James V created the College of Justice in 1532, granting it judicial power, 'to sitt and decyde apone all actiouns civile'. Alexander Mylne, Abbot of Cambuskenneth, was appointed as the first president of this new legal institution.

MARY OF GUISE AT STIRLING

Mary Queen of Scots came to the throne even younger than her father had, aged just six days old.

After her coronation in 1543, parliament renounced an alliance with England, which would have meant the young queen marrying Henry VIII's son, Edward.

This led Henry to initiate the 'Rough Wooing' in 1544, which saw seven years of destructive English invasions.

Below An artist's impression of Mary of Guise relaxing with courtiers in the Queen's Inner Hall.

Mary and her mother, Mary of Guise, remained safe within the stronghold of Stirling Castle until the young queen was sent to France in 1548. She was to live at the French royal court to prepare her for marriage to François, the dauphin, heir to the French throne.

Mary of Guise remained at Stirling, holding court in the absence of her daughter the queen. She left Scotland only once, spending a year in France in 1550–1. She spent much of that time with her daughter and with François, her son by her first marriage, who died during her visit.

In 1554 she became regent of Scotland, governing the country until the year before her death. Supported by French money and French troops, she was responsible for commissioning major artillery defences at Stirling Castle, including the French Spur, to the east of the main entrance.

During her regency Mary tried to quell the rise of Protestantism, which saw riots and the destruction of churches, including Cambuskenneth Abbey. Religious tensions remained high at the time of her death in Edinburgh in 1560.

Right Mary of Guise in later life, in a portrait by the French court artist François Clouet.

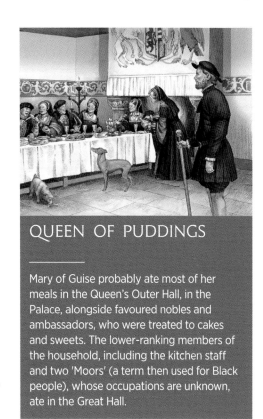

QUEEN OF PUDDINGS

Mary of Guise probably ate most of her meals in the Queen's Outer Hall, in the Palace, alongside favoured nobles and ambassadors, who were treated to cakes and sweets. The lower-ranking members of the household, including the kitchen staff and two 'Moors' (a term then used for Black people), whose occupations are unknown, ate in the Great Hall.

MARY QUEEN OF SCOTS AND DARNLEY

In 1561 Mary returned from France, where she had been queen alongside her first husband, François II, who died in 1560. She based herself mainly at Holyrood, just outside Edinburgh, but also spent time at her childhood home of Stirling.

In 1565, Mary married her second husband, Henry Stewart, Lord Darnley. Their son, James, was born the following year. Mary put on a dazzling show for his baptism in the old Chapel Royal. Cannon, gunpowder, and saltpetre were hauled up to the castle by night, 'for feir of knawlege thairof' – to maximise their surprise impact.

The fireworks display took place at the end of three days of banquets, masques and a mock siege of a temporary fortress built on what is now the site of the Esplanade.

The atmosphere was tense, as the previous year several of Mary's nobles had murdered Mary's secretary, David Riccio. Many of them were Protestant and refused to attend the Catholic service, including Darnley. But the theme was one of reconciliation, with the Riccio conspirators pardoned and Catholics and Protestants dining together.

1 A rare silver coin, minted in 1565, shows the heads of both Mary and Darnley. Darnley's ambitions to be recognised as joint monarch were ended by his violent death in 1567.
2 Double portrait of Mary Queen of Scots and her second husband Henry, Lord Darnley, around 1565.

Mary charged the Earl and Countess of Mar, John Erskine and Annabella Murray, with looking after James at Stirling. He was 'to be conservit, nurist and upbrocht within our said Castell of Striviling under your tutill and governance'. The Erskine family had been keepers of Stirling Castle since as far back as the mid-1300s.

In 1567 Mary arrived to take her son to Edinburgh, but the Mars stuck to their original orders and refused to allow his removal. This was the last time Mary saw James. A few months later, she was forced to abdicate, and the following year she escaped to England, never to return.

JAMES VI AND ANNA OF DENMARK

Mary's son, James VI, spent his entire childhood at Stirling Castle, not leaving until 1579.

The young king lived a life of protected luxury, with six ladies to rock his cradle, two of whom also changed his nappies. James affectionately called the Mars 'Lord Deddy' and 'Lady Minny', and Countess Annabella slept in James's room until he was 11.

James received a rigorous education at Stirling alongside other boys including the Mars' son, John. His tutors, George Buchanan and Peter Young, taught them French, Latin, and Greek, as well as history, rhetoric, moral philosophy, and the Protestant religion.

Buchanan saw the ideal monarch as a servant of the people, whose power could be removed if they acted unjustly. But in James's own later publications, he asserted his rights as a divinely appointed monarch.

James's queen, Anna of Denmark, gave birth to their first child, Henry Frederick, at Stirling in 1594.

The baby was baptised in the newly rebuilt Chapel Royal (see pages 98–99). This elaborate occasion, attended by foreign ambassadors, was celebrated with a tournament and a banquet.

Henry's care was entrusted to Annabella and her son, John, 2nd Earl of Mar. Queen Anna was deeply unhappy about this arrangement, but Henry remained at Stirling with the Mars until 1603, when the court relocated to London. At this separation, Henry 'burst forth into tears'.

Henry died in 1612 and his brother Charles became heir to the throne. Charles I briefly visited Stirling Castle in 1633, in preparation for which Valentine Jenkin repainted the Chapel Royal, the Great Hall, and the Palace. Charles was the last reigning monarch to stay at the castle.

1 King James VI, later James I of England.
2 Queen Anna of Demark.
3 Their firstborn son, Prince Henry.
4 Their younger son, who succeeded as King Charles I.

97

ERICVS · HENRI
G · PRINCEPS ·
VM · ÆTATIS ·
· 1 · 9 · 6 ·

1

2

3

4

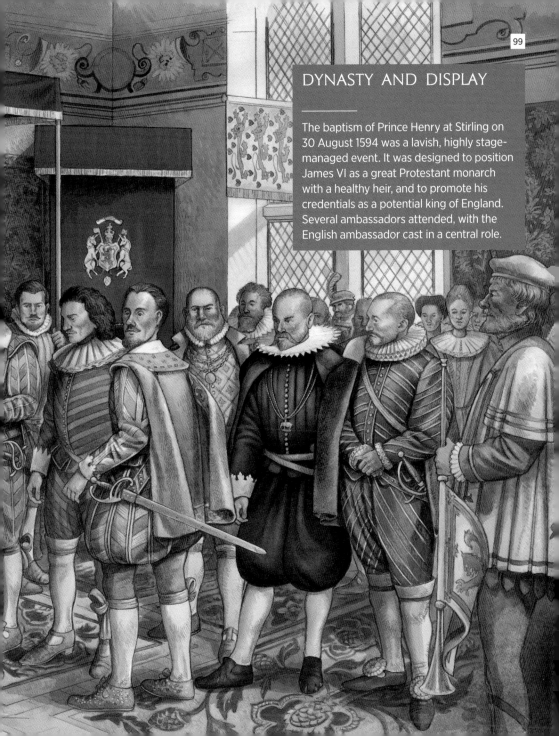

DYNASTY AND DISPLAY

The baptism of Prince Henry at Stirling on 30 August 1594 was a lavish, highly stage-managed event. It was designed to position James VI as a great Protestant monarch with a healthy heir, and to promote his credentials as a potential king of England. Several ambassadors attended, with the English ambassador cast in a central role.

STIRLING IN THE JACOBITE ERA

Although the monarch was based in London from 1603, royal politics continued to affect Stirling Castle. In 1688 James VII was forced into exile due to his unpopular Catholic faith. He was replaced as monarch by his Protestant daughter, Mary, and her husband, William of Orange.

This led to decades of warfare between supporters of James and his descendants, known as Jacobites, on one side, and supporters of Mary and her successors on the other. Jacobite risings occurred in 1689, 1708, 1715, 1719, and 1745.

The abortive rising of 1708 was largely a reaction to the 1707 Acts of Union, by which Scotland became part of the United Kingdom. It prompted a major redevelopment of the castle's Outer Defences, originally built for Mary of Guise. A deep ditch was constructed, with a caponier, or covered shooting gallery, defending the west end and artillery emplacements at the east.

The accession of George I, a distant German relation of the Stuarts, in 1714 helped to provoke the 1715 rising. This was led by John Erskine, 6th Earl of Mar and hereditary governor of Stirling Castle. Mar fought for Prince James, son of James VII, at Sheriffmuir, near Stirling, but support was dwindling and the rising ended in Mar's forfeiture and exile. While living in Paris, he redesigned Stirling Castle Palace, but he never returned to Scotland to carry out these plans.

In 1745 the Jacobite cause was revived by Prince James's son Charles, known as 'Bonnie Prince Charlie'. After military advances as far south as Derby in the English Midlands, in 1746 his forces retreated through Scotland. They besieged Stirling Castle, but failed to take it, then retreated further. They were finally defeated at Culloden, near Inverness.

1 Queen Mary II with her husband and joint monarch, William of Orange.
2 John Erskine, Earl of Mar, who led the Jacobite Rising of 1715. Later, in exile, he produced designs for the remodelling of Stirling Castle that were never implemented.
3 William Blakeney, governor of Stirling Castle during the Jacobite siege of 1746.

JANE FERRIER

Jane Graham, née Ferrier, published her drawings of the Stirling Heads in *Lacunar Strevelinense* (1817).

Many of the Heads had been dispersed and some were even said to have been used by boys in hoop rolling and by bakers to heat their ovens. Jane recognised their artistic and historic value and preserved their appearance in her skilful drawings.

Jane lived at the castle, where her husband, General Samuel Graham, was deputy governor. She was well-connected in literary circles. Her novelist sister Susan Ferrier may have written *Destiny* (1831) while staying at the castle. Jane was also acquainted with Robert Burns, who referred to the sisters as 'rhyme-inspiring lasses', and Walter Scott, who asked the Grahams to show his son around the castle, 'connected as it is with so many noble reminiscences'.

1 One of Jane Ferrier's drawings of the Stirling Heads.
2 A portrait of Jane Ferrier.

THE RADICAL WAR OF 1820

By 1820 a radical political group had emerged seeking a universal franchise for men, annual parliaments, and the repeal of the 1707 Acts of Union. Unrest was worsened by economic hardship and unemployment among artisans.

Participants in an armed insurrection were intercepted and captured on their way to attack the Carron Iron Works near Falkirk. They had been betrayed by a spy, John King.

Below Weapons used by participants during the Radical War.

They were held prisoner at Stirling Castle, under General Graham, and 88 were charged with high treason. Of these, 22 were transported to the penal colonies but weavers John Baird and Andrew Hardie, two of the leaders, were sentenced to death.

Thousands attended their execution in front of Stirling Jail on Broad Street. Both claimed to stand for 'the cause of truth and justice'. They were hanged then their heads were severed and displayed to the sympathetic crowd.

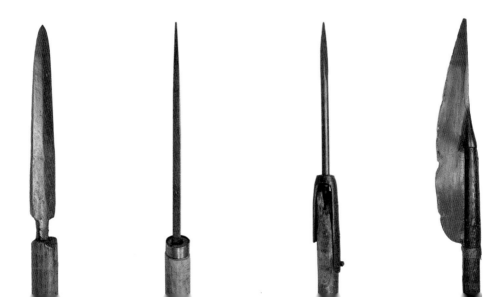

MODERN TIMES

In the period after the Jacobite Risings, Stirling Castle served as both a military base and a tourist attraction.

In the later 1700s, buildings at the castle were converted to accommodate troops. The Great Hall and the Chapel Royal were subdivided to provide barracks, a dining hall, a schoolroom and storage space. The Palace and King's Old Building were also used.

Further military buildings were added, including the Main Guard House and the Fort Major's House. The Argyll and Sutherland Highlanders, formed in 1881, were headquartered at the castle until 2006.

Meanwhile, Stirling became a destination for travellers and writers. Dorothy Wordsworth, diarist and sister of the poet, noted in 1803 that 'The architecture of a part of the Castle is very fine, and the whole building in good repair: some parts, indeed, are modern.' But by 1822, on a second visit, Wordsworth noted that birds nested 'within the decaying walls'.

Yorkshire landowner Anne Lister visited in 1828 with her lover Sibella Maclean. Lister described the castle as 'All converted into barracks & stores & Lieutenant General Grey's (the governor) house. The depot of the 42nd highland regiment.' The Chapel Royal was in use as an armoury, but still contained a pulpit said to have been used by John Knox, though he died before the existing chapel was built.

In 1906 guardianship of the castle was transferred to the Office of Works, a predecessor of Historic Environment Scotland. This meant that it would be preserved and protected as a valuable part of the nation's heritage.

1 Stirling Castle features in a recruitment poster of 1914.
2 The occasion in 2011 of the Laying Up of the Last Stand of Argyll Colours by their successors, the 5th Battalion, The Royal Regiment of Scotland.

2

RECREATING THE PALACE

Now in the care of Historic Environment Scotland, the castle has undergone significant recreation and reconstruction work in recent decades.

Between the 1960s and the 2010s, several buildings around the Inner Close were returned to how they might have looked in the 1500s.

The hammerbeam roof of James IV's Great Hall has been recreated and its exterior harling and limewash reapplied. The interior of the Palace has been decorated and furnished in a way historically accurate to the time of James V and Mary of Guise. And interior paintwork in the Chapel Royal, dating back to James VI's reign, has been restored.

Peopled by expert costumed interpreters, these recreated spaces show just how bright and vibrant the Scottish court once was.

This page Specialist artists at work on the decoration of the Palace in 2010. The Stirling Heads were painted after being fixed to the ceiling of the King's Inner Hall.

FURTHER READING

- Ishbel C. M. Barnes, *Janet Kennedy, Royal Mistress: Marriage and Divorce at the Courts of James IV and V* (Edinburgh, 2007)
- Fiona Downie, *She is but a Woman: Queenship in Scotland, 1424–1463* (Edinburgh, 2006)
- Gordon Ewart and Dennis Gallagher (eds), *With Thy Towers High: The Archaeology of Stirling Castle and Palace* (Edinburgh, 2015)
- Richard Fawcett (ed.), *Stirling Castle: The Restoration of the Great Hall* (York, 2001)
- John Gifford, Frank Arneil Walker and Richard Fawcett, *Stirling and Central Scotland, Buildings of Scotland* (New Haven and London, 2002)
- John G. Harrison, *Rebirth of a Palace: The Royal Court at Stirling Castle* (Edinburgh, 2011)
- Michael Penman, *Robert the Bruce, King of the Scots,* 2nd ed (New Haven and London, 2018)
- Steven J. Reid, *The Early Life of James VI: A Long Apprenticeship, 1566–1585* (Edinburgh, 2023)
- Edward M. Spiers, Jeremy A. Crang and Matthew J. Strickland (eds), *A Military History of Scotland* (Edinburgh, 2014)

CREDITS

This edition first published by Historic Environment Scotland, 2024
Printed from sustainable materials
© Historic Environment Scotland 2024
ISBN 978-1-84917-303-2

Historic Environment Scotland
Scottish Charity No. SC045925

Principal Office
Longmore House, Salisbury Place, Edinburgh EH9 1SH

Authors Andrew Burnet and Morvern French
Design ABG Design
Photography Historic Environment Scotland Photo Unit

Illustrations
p.4 and p.64 Yvonne Holton
p.6, p.20, p.26, p.57, pp.70–1, pp.82–3, p.88, p.92, p.93 and pp.98–9 David Lawrence
p.12 and p.40 David Simon
p.72 Bob Marshall

We are grateful to PhD candidate Charlie Spragg, University of Edinburgh, for contributing her research to the illustration of Prince Henry's baptism (pp. 98–99); and to the family of the Earl of Rosebery for allowing us to photograph the portrait of Prince Henry (p.67 and p.96)

All images © Historic Environment Scotland/© Crown copyright, reproduced by courtesy of HES, except: **front cover:** © Martin Valigursky | Dreamstime.com; **p.4, p.64 cl and p.78 t** © National Museums Scotland. Licensor www.scran.ac.uk; **p.5 t, p.81 and p.86** © National Library of Scotland. Licensor www.scran.ac.uk; **p.59** Art Collection/Alamy Stock Photo; **p.6 l and p.97 tl** © National Galleries of Scotland. Licensor www.scran.ac.uk; **p.6 c and p.67 bl** Bridgeman Images; **p.16** Travel Scotland—Paul White/ Alamy Stock Photo; **p.41, p.42 t, p.43 t & c, p.44, p.45, p.66 bl and p.67 br** Museum of the Argyll and Sutherland Highlanders; **p.49** © Leonard de Selva/ Bridgeman Images; **pp.56–57** © Smith Museum & Art Gallery, Stirling; **p.58** © Getty Museum, acquired in honor of Thomas Kren; **p.60** © Earl of Mar and Kellie. Licensor www.scran.ac.uk; **p.64 bl, p.67 tr and p.97 br** © National Trust for Scotland. Licensor www.scran.ac.uk; **p.64 c** Stuttgart, Wuerttembergische Landesbibliothek, Cod. hist. qt. 141, p. 97; **p.65 t** © British Library Board. All Rights Reserved/Bridgeman Images; **p.65 cr** © Austrian National Library, 245 Bll. Seitennummer 243v; **p.65 bl, p.66 t and p.66 cl** © Scottish National Portrait Gallery. Licensor www.scran.ac.uk; **p.67 cl** Reproduced with the permission of the National Library of Scotland; **p.67 cr and p.101 tr** © Scottish National Portrait Gallery; **p.72** © Bob Marshall; **p.73** Photo 12/Universal Images Group via Getty Images; **p.74 t** Niday Picture Library/Alamy Stock Photo; **p.74 b** The Bodleian Libraries, University of Oxford, C 292; folio 105r; **p.75** © Look and Learn/Bridgeman Images; **p.79** Lebrecht Authors/Bridgeman Images; **p. 5 r and pp.84–5** © The Royal Collection 2023, His Majesty King Charles III. Licensor www.scran.ac.uk; **p.91** Art Collection 2/Alamy Stock Photo; **p.93** © The Trustees of the British Museum; **p.94** © The Trustees of the British Museum. Licensor www.scran.ac.uk; **p.95** National Trust Photographic Library/Bridgeman Images; **p.97 tr** © Philip Mould Historical Portraits Image Library; **p.100 and p.101 b** © National Portrait Gallery, London; **p.104** © Imperial War Museum (Art.IWM PST 12148)

l (left); r (right); c (centre); t (top); b (bottom)

STIRLING CASTLE AT A GLANCE

1 Esplanade
Formed in 1809 to create a military parade ground and an impressive, level approach to the castle.

2 Outer Defences
Built in the early 1700s in response to the threat of civil war with the Jacobites.

3 Guardroom Square
A cobbled courtyard where a stable block of the 1800s now serves as the shop and ticket office.

4 Forework
The impressive remnant of a once much taller, four-towered entranceway commissioned around 1500 by James IV.

5 Queen Anne Garden
Established at least 500 years ago.

6 Castle Exhibition
An introduction to the castle's long and colourful story.

7 Outer Close
The lower and more accessible of the castle's two main enclosures.

8 Palace
Built in the 1530s–40s as a residence for James V and Mary of Guise, the Palace has been recreated as it may have looked when first completed.

9 Inner Close
The castle's upper courtyard, this was the focus of royal life at Stirling.

10 King's Old Building
Built as a private residence for King James IV, and now housing the regimental museum of the Argyll and Sutherland Highlanders.

11 Great Hall
Scotland's largest and grandest banqueting hall, built around 1500 as a venue for feasts and state occasions.

12 Chapel Royal
Built in 1594 to host the spectacular baptism of Prince Henry, heir to the throne.

13 Douglas Garden
A secluded space at the rock's highest point, where visitors can access a wall-walk with spectacular views.

14 Great Kitchens
Built around 1500 to prepare banquets for the Great Hall; now reconstructed to show cooks hard at work.

15 North Gate
The oldest standing structure in the castle, with parts dating from the 1380s.

16 Nether Bailey
The lowest enclosure in the castle, containing service buildings and munitions stores.

17 Tapestry Exhibition
Discover the story of the Stirling Tapestries in the purpose-built studio where some of them were woven.

18 King's And Queen's Knots
Geometrical raised gardens below the castle, created in the 1620s, on the site of earlier gardens.

Toilets
Café
Shop